Praying
with
Pictures

By the same author

Borrowing the Eyes of Others: Reflecting with Paintings, Volume 1
Awakening to Yourself: Reflecting with Paintings, Volume 2
Journeying with Jesus: a Companion's Guide
Journeying with Jesus: a Companion's Guide for Groups
Where Does the Jesus Story Begin?
Waiting on God
Jesus and the Gospels
Seasons of the Word: Reflections on the Sunday Readings
The Parables of Jesus
Impressions of Jesus
The Gospel of Mark
The Gospel of Luke
Emmaus: the Gracious Visit of God

Reflecting with Paintings – set of 15 reflections on CD
Where Does the Jesus Story Begin? – set of 10 lectures on CD
Jesus and the Gospels – set of 36 lectures on CD

www.denismcbride.com

Praying
with
Pictures

Denis McBride

A Redemptorist Publication

Praying
with Pictures

Denis McBride

Copyright © Redemptorist Publications, 2010

Published by **Redemptorist Publications**
A Registered Charity limited by guarantee. Registered in England 3261721.

First published February 2010

Design by Louise Hilton, Attica Design
Photography: iStock and Shutterstock

ISBN 978-0-85231-372-5

A CIP catalogue record for this book is available from the British Library.

Printed by Lithgo Press Limited, Leicester LE8 6NU

Redemptorist
PUBLICATIONS

Alphonsus House Chawton Hampshire GU34 3HQ
Telephone 01420 88222   01420 88805
rp@rpbooks.co.uk   www.rpbooks.co.uk

For the staff of Redemptorist Publications,
in affection, in respect, in gratitude

How to pray   8-15

Prayers

Contents

How to pray

Dear Reader,

Welcome to this book of praying with pictures, a gathering of prayers from a wide variety of voices. I hope you enjoy it, and that sometimes it annoys you! Listening to people who are different from us, struggling to find words for what they're going through, can either make us retreat into our own corner or force us beyond ourselves, to think again. Whose prayers would *you* listen to attentively? Whose prayers, if any, would you instinctively ignore?

Personal prayer is simple; it is also challenging: being ourselves before our God while allowing God to be God. Two different "presences" come together to forge a relationship of mutual caring.

Intimacy can frighten us at the best of times, and we can be shy of being ourselves in prayer as we can with those we trust. We're ever alert to signs of disapproval, wariness, shuffling. Should we adjust or carry on?

Personal prayer is a meeting between two lovers, each longing to be closer to one another. It's a coming together, to talk and to listen, to understand and, hopefully, to grasp the beauty and complexity of each other. If we want to be known for who we are, nervous about being misrepresented, it's a safe bet that God wants the same.

In our prayer the challenge is to be real, truthful, heartfelt, unaffected.

There is little point in dressing up before the one who knows us better than we could ever know ourselves. And when we pray regularly, at least God can't pretend he doesn't know us.

In personal prayer we approach the God of all mercies without make-up or disguise, without mask or pretence, hoping to find an expression for who we are and what we're facing in life. Personal prayer is not performance; it is the language of real life.

Take an example from Saint Paul: the apostle pleads with God in prayer to take away his newly discovered weaknesses, which seriously embarrass him as a perfectionist. For someone who has never once disobeyed the law, who has been a Pharisee to outclass all other Pharisees, this new discovery is deeply unsettling. But God's declared response reveals to Paul that his request is refused, and he will have to learn to live with weaknesses all the days of his life. There is a pastoral purpose in all this: to stop Paul from becoming too proud.

"Whose prayers would *you* listen to attentively?"

"I will be very happy to make my weaknesses my special boast"

You then watch Paul make a dramatic shift, suddenly explaining to his now bewildered readers: "I will be very happy to make my weaknesses my special boast, so that the power of Christ may stay over me." How about that for a spectacular change of perspective? How about that for the power of prayer?

Paul doesn't try to hide from God, although previous to this he'd always suspected that God had no truck with weakness, desiring only flawless performance. Paul now knows he will never justify himself but will need God's mercy every day of his life. In the light of his personal prayer Paul now shares an utterly stunning revelation: not only that weaknesses are no obstacle to God's love but that God's glory can shine through them. Indeed it might be true to say that God is a lot more skilled, more practised, at accepting our weaknesses than we are.

Personal prayer is neither a litany of alleluias nor a shopping list of petitions: prayer is much more nuanced and can take many forms. As in the great book of the Psalms,

"Nothing about us is excluded from prayer"

prayer can be a scream or an endless groan, a grievance for some slight or hurt; it might be an angry complaint or an accusation; it could be a thank-you note for a loved one or for a special grace that has been granted; it could be delicious praise, shyly made.

The treasure book of the Psalms teaches us that we should pray always, no matter what. Whatever mood or condition we are in, whatever is happening in our life, we keep in touch with the God who is slow to anger and rich in graciousness. Nothing about us is excluded from prayer.

One of the great privileges of being a priest is to listen to people who come "just for a chat" – which often turns into a struggle to be real about themselves, their relationships, their aspirations. They come not to discuss projects or plans or business – thank God for that! – but to find a voice for what is happening in their lives and what they think is really going on.

After sitting down and carefully adjusting something that doesn't need adjusting, they begin by commenting on the fitfulness of the weather or the colour of the curtains – anything except what

they've come to talk about. That's okay: we all need time to gather our confidence and point ourselves in the right direction. You wait for a gentle break in the nervous flow of small talk to ask Jesus' risky question: "What do you want me to do for you?"

The story then begins cautiously, often in a roundabout way, as the person heads for the destination. You pay attention to the pauses, the rephrasing, the uncertainty, the guesses, the sudden breaths. You taste the awkward silences. The body language tells its own story. At times you might wonder

what kind of God they believe in and how they got to this point. You resist interrupting, clarifying, filling in. You try your best to stay focused without thinking about Brother Anthony's soup. You cannot help but admire the heroic effort to be frank and the resolve to get it all out.

You try to give this person your best thinking while respecting ambiguity and confusion. You refuse to write their script or pretend that you have some exclusive hotline to God that will guarantee a quick fix to their problems. You stay humble before such huge honesty and try to honour it, yes, with your

"Prayer
    pushes us out,
beyond ourselves,
    into the deep"

own. You remind yourself that you are supposed to proclaim Good News, not just orthodoxy, so you make a real effort to ask the right questions, understand the issues, broaden the canvas, and, together, seek a way forward.

These times are very close to prayer.

And I know, dear reader, that soon I will be in that other chair when I visit my ancient wise mentor. And he will ask me, after the usual entrance rites and a double gin and small tonic: "So tell me, Denis, how are things?"

And then it will be my turn to tell the story, find delicate words, pause, rephrase, correct, try, with as much honesty as I can muster, to relate the truth about myself. Not easy. But we all need someone with whom to be real before God, as a practice for prayer.

Prayer, of course, is not just about ourselves, transfixed by our own agenda in a free counselling session with God. We are expected to have a place in our prayer and in our lives for those who are poor or lonely, those who feel rejected or forgotten, for all the people who feel hurt by life and have no one to support them. Prayer is not only being open to God about ourselves but bothering God about the peripheral people. Prayer pushes us out, beyond ourselves, into the deep.

In the following prayers I have tried to find a voice for all sorts of people and situations, just as I have listened to the stories of all sorts of people in all sorts of situations. I still hear their voices in the night, the echoes of those wonderfully varied accents, which I have tried to recapture in these prayers. To them, much thanks.

Finally, dear reader, if it's true to say that most people think in pictures rather than in words, I've chosen a selection of photographs to provide images to support the prayers. As you turn the pages the photographs might stir you to go in a totally different direction from mine, and make your own prayers in your own words. That, of course, would be great! Whatever happens, I hope this little book will help you understand that you can pray no matter what condition you're in, no matter how you feel: we pray always, keeping in touch with our beloved God.

Sincerely,

Denis McBride, C.Ss.R.
Alphonsus House
Chawton
Hampshire
GU34 3HQ

May the blessing

of the road be upon me
and all I meet.

May I make new friends
as I travel onwards,
and confront few enemies.

Let it be that one day
I fall in love, mightily,
and that this love
will be my tall tower
as I will be its stronghold
for ever and a day.

Amen.

I was a high-flyer once, Lord,

and my friends would rib me and say
that the angels must have taken notes:
how my wings hovered and swooped
and rose and then, somehow,
appeared stilled, motionless,
suspended between heaven and earth.

No high-flyer should have a permanent address;
but now my gypsy heart is forever grounded,
stationed, earthed, rooted.
All those faraway places
and people and sounds
have now melted into memory.

But what a memory, Lord!
I know I look weary and worn and wounded,
but I have been to the top of the world
and frolicked with angels!
I am filled with gratitude for the life I have lived,
for the people I have learned to love,
for the multitude of places I landed,
and for the few I found hard to leave.

Thanks, Lord, for the life you have led me.

Now in the stillness lead me on
into the fullness of your presence.

Amen.

Do I look unhappy to you, Lord, radically incomplete?

The things people say to me and the questions
I get asked because I tell people I am happily single!
Why does that puzzle, even annoy, so many?

> "You'll meet someone soon, don't worry."
> "Maybe you should see a doctor?"
> "Are you gay or something?"
> "You hate men, I guess. Can't blame you, dear."
> "But you're beautiful, with perfect teeth! I don't get it."
> "Vocation, right? Are you a nun-in-waiting?"
> "You're a sex maniac who can't commit!"
> "Shame you're asexual – no idea what you're missing!"

I spend half my life covering my ears, Lord,
to the questions and the unwanted advice.
People presume that I must be a bit loony
because I say I'm content the way I am.
Very few people actually listen to me,
caught up in their own hunger and needs:
I seem to be beyond the reach of their indulgence.

> I am happy the way I am and I love my life.
> I come from a loving family, have pots of friends,
> and a fulfilling job. I feel really lucky.
> And I'm not a selfish witch, devoted only to me.

Dear Lord, help people to understand
the beauty of diversity and that sometimes
other people are *other*, different from them.
As someone who was happily single yourself,
can you please help people get it? I'm so tired.

In a world

where survival depends
so much on being alert and agile,
thank you, Lord,
for the dozy moments in life.

Dear Lord,

at dinner tonight my grandchildren
told me with great excitement
that I am no longer an old woman
but a "senior lady" – according to
something called Health and Safety.

I don't know who Health and Safety are –
probably a new rock group –
but I told them that I'm very happy
being what I am – an old woman
with a face like the Dead Sea Scrolls.
They laughed and hooted!

Dear Lord, aside from everything,
may you protect and bless
all those I love,
and attend with kindness
those I do not.

Those I have hurt,
I kneel before for blessing.
From those I have failed,
I beg humble pardon.

To those who have loved me
long and well
through my ancient days,
I wish with all my heart
fullness of life
and peace everlasting.

Amen.

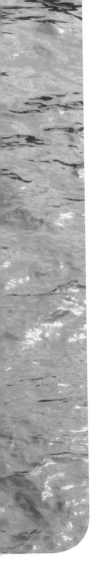

It's morning and here I am again, Lord,

my usual spot, on the bank of the Seine,
coming around slowly to this new day,
hoping that this might be the day – who knows? –
when I can leave behind the self I need to outgrow,
turn towards the ancient dream you had of me.

You know I'm an expert in avoiding myself,
acting out a pleasing drama for others.
You know, Lord, how everyone thinks
I'm charming and agreeable, docile and polite –
Mr Inoffensive – albeit
with a gravitational pull towards boredom.
This I realise; this I have been given to know.
Haven't I overhead people whisper knowingly
that I will never set the heather alight?
Clearly I don't have the X factor.

People might want me around them,
but I feel they don't want me.

At least, not as I am now.
Give me courage, Lord,
to rise like the dawn to greet
the stranger that is my true self.
Let me ignore him no longer
but embrace him as the dream you thought lost
since the foundation of the world.

In coming home to myself, Lord,
may I meet you for the first time.

FOR THE COURAGE TO BE YOURSELF

For our beautiful and bruised earth

I pray to you, creator of all things.

Grant that we might reverence
what we take for granted
and learn to honour
what we now spoil.

Awaken in us a wonder
for the earth we have inherited
from your providence.
May our care and attention
be partners in the growth
of your world,
now and always.

Amen.

"This is the day the Lord has made;

let us rejoice and be glad in it."

Help me, Lord, to greet this morning
as your gift of a new day –
not just the extension of yesterday.

Yesterday was everlasting muddle;
nothing was right; zilch was achieved;
my best efforts died without notice.
Nobody attended the funeral.

Some days, I guess, neither who we are
nor what we struggle to achieve
seems wanted by anyone.
Even you might feel like that, Lord?

May today rise above yesterday
as the sun will surely soar above
this field of mist, this everlasting fence.

Awaken me, Lord, to your unfenced wonder.
And at the close of this day,
may I know why you gave it to me.

It's quiet in the house now, Lord.

I've read the kids to the land of slumber as usual,
and they're tucked up for the night
after whispering goodnight to their guardian angels.
Harry reckons that his guardian angel has toothache,
so he's holding back from asking any big favours.
He explained to me with great solemnity:
"Dad, I won't bother him right now
cos even angels need a break sometimes, right?"

I love this time of quiet, Lord,
just me, the garden, the night, and you.
I always look back over the day,
not to hug my achievements or confess my failures,
but to count my many blessings.

For my wife, Siobhan, whom I do not deserve,
I thank you with a full heart this night and every night.
For our three kids, Harry, Jack, and Marie –
as different as they are impossible –
no words can capture my thankfulness.
They have reintroduced me to wonder,
to reverence before life,
to the joy of sharing daft stories.

Thanks, Lord, for the gift of ordinary time,
for the quiet rhythm of family life
and the dramatic upsets,
and for all we fail to be grateful for, day and night.
Let me never take for granted the gift of any day.

AT THE END OF THE DAY

"To every thing there is a season,

and a time to every purpose under heaven."

Where does time go to, Lord?
You know what we often say:
"There's plenty of it when you don't need it
and none when you do."

When we're young, we feel immortal,
with time on our side, endlessly ahead of us.
Then, as we get older, we hear the ticking…
As I know now from experience:
the frustrating thing about the past is
that the longer we live, there's more of it!
As our past gets longer, our future gets shorter
and we begin to consider the time we have left.

How we talk about time so much:
"Why don't you take more time?"
"There was a time when you had time for me."
"It's time to let go and move on."
"Have you got a few minutes to spare?"
"It's only a matter of time."
"We had the time of our life!"
"Sorry, my dear, but time's up."

I know we can't buy time, borrow time,
save time, spend time, cheat time, kill time.
Can you please help us, Lord, to cherish
whatever time, in your wisdom, you grant us?

Tomorrow may not be another day.

TO CHERISH THE TIME WE HAVE

Every day,
for sure, Lord,
somebody tells me

that I'm happy only when I'm miserable –
the original grumpy old man who's grown
to look like the mournful British bulldog.

But I bet you get crotchety sometimes, Lord,
when you see what's happening
around the bonny world you've created.

Do you ever get weary of religion, Lord,
bored stiff with all the dressing up,
the processions and the genuflections,
all that singing and squawking and stuff?
Are you really big on incense?

For you, does the beauty of liturgy
compensate for the wretchedness of war?
Do the Mozart motets win out over
the wailing of those brutally unhoused?

What are your ears attuned to, Lord?
Which prayers pierce the clouds?
What really gets to you?

Who are you listening to now?
Do I have a chance of being heard, Lord,
without showering you with alleluias?

This is not a big confession or anything
but, to be straightforward with you,
I'm not really an alleluia man…
Hope you have a wee space for the likes of me
in your Father's house of many rooms.

TO BE HEARD AS YOURSELF

I lost my innocence, Lord,

when you took my son away from me.
Up to that hour, I believed and I prayed,
I worshipped and I sang: faith was effortless.
My favourite Gospel verse described you well:
"A light that shines in the dark,
a light that darkness cannot overpower."

> When we buried Paulito, the darkness won out,
> and I buried my faith alongside him.
> For one who was loved so much,
> his coffin weighed so little.
> The young Scottish priest had no idea –
> how could he? – that he was presiding
> over a double funeral that day.
> "They closed the tomb and all withdrew."

Now darkness has seeped into everything.
Now I feel like I'm on my knees,
searching among the ruins of a cathedral
for the thin wafer of your presence, Lord.
My knees are raw, my fingers numb.

> His absence is so much larger than yours, Lord.

Paulito recorded our family message
on the answerphone: "Hi, folks,
no one home. Leave a message
and we'll get back to you real soon."
The wee soul practised so hard to get it right.

> Now I keep phoning home to hear his voice
> and I always leave a message.
> How dumb is that, Lord?
> Useless as prayer…

ON THE DEATH OF A CHILD

"Put out into the deep."

I'm at home in the shallows, Lord,
forever paddling around
within safe distance of the lakeside.
I heard your call to leave familiar shores
and test myself in the deep; so I surprised myself,
threw caution to the wind, hooded myself
against the elements, and rowed like a madman.

So here I am plumbing the depths,
scared what the deep might give up.
What if I can't handle what might surface
from way down there? My little canoe,
as you can see, has no room for a large catch.
I mean if I cough I could capsize...

You know that I'm shy, awkward, wooden,
really desperate around most people.
I never know what to say after mumbling, "Hello" –
my eyes hunting around the room for an exit.
My girlfriend, who could talk the head off a donkey,
says that in company I'm charisma-free.
She loves me, I know, because I never interrupt
her effortless everlasting flow of words.

One thing I have to admit, for sure, Lord:
out here I feel somehow closer to you,
maybe because, like Jonah, I'm out of my element?
Does fear nudge you closer to faith?
I know, Lord, you have something in mind for me;
but could you be nice, please, and let me know
without heaving me overboard, into the deep,
to keep an appointment with a passing whale?

Thanks, Lord. Can I go home now?

Jock took this pic of me, Lord,

and you have to admit it's totally gorgeous,
but you can guess it wasn't taken in Scotland!
We've been going steady for eight months now
and I love him to distraction, apart from the beard.

The differences between us are huge.
Jock is a Scottish engineer (atheist);
I am a Filipino psychiatric nurse (Catholic, of course).

Where I express what I want,
he fastens on what needs to be done.
Where I am imaginative, he is logical and linear.
Where I love drama, he prefers procedure.
Where I dream options, he selects a planned route.
Where I want to be happy, he needs to be right.
Where I love largesse, he admires frugality.
While I accept ambiguity, he demands clarity.
While I like spontaneity, he wants to be proper.

While I share feeling, he emits impenetrable signals.
While I make mistakes, he avoids error.
While I admire creativity, he respects self-discipline.
Where I focus on relationships, he fixes on work.

> Is there any hope for us, Lord?
> Can the highlands of Scotland marry
> the mountains of Baguio?
> Tell me, Lord, please, that you still do miracles!

We pray
for the Church

throughout the world:
renew your people in love
for you and one another.
Cleanse us and revive us;
enlighten us and empower us;
may you prosper all that we do
for the sake of your name.

Grant pardon for the ways
we have sinned and diminished
your light in the world.
For this, we plead for mercy.

You are greater than our weakness,
stronger than our fall from grace:
refresh and fortify us anew
so that the beauty of the Gospel
will be heard in the words we speak
and recognised in all that we do.

We pray with your apostle Paul:
that the good work you began in us
will be brought to its completion.

Amen.

FOR THE UNIVERSAL CHURCH

This is the nearest
I come, Lord,

to your house, the nearest I dare come.
It was on holiday here, three years ago,
that I decided to abort the child in my womb.
It sounds the strangest thing to admit now,
but it all seemed so reasonable at the time.
"Honest, love," he said, "it really is for the best.
It's the tidiest solution all round. Believe me."

Now he has disappeared, the child is for ever gone,
and I'm on my own, revisiting a large absence.

There are some decisions that can never be unmade,
none more irreversible than the one we made that day.
I let go of the gift of life, Lord,
for the sake of... tidiness...

Now, although my body has healed, Lord,
my soul is covered in wounds that will never mend.
I pray not for myself but for my rejected child.
May you hold him tight and let him know
that he is wanted and loved, after all.
Please reassure him that there is a place
reserved for him since the foundation of the world
in the home of your bountiful heart.
My heart, sadly, was too small.

Tell him I learned to love him too late,
but that my love for him
is the most precious thing I have,
the only jewel I will ever wear.

FOR A REJECTED BABY

When my twin sister took this pic, Lord,

she told me to dump my usual brooding self.
"Smile, Kevin," she shouted, "do it just for me!"
What do you think? Not bad. I'm really pleased
and might upload it as my profile pic on Facebook.
Anyway, you don't need the pic to recognise me.

Tell me this, Lord: did you ever feel that
who you really were was not what was wanted?
That your preferences and point of view
somehow attracted instinctive disapproval?
You didn't even have to say anything, just turn up!
Bet you never had your Father say to you:
"Son, I like you but not what you are."

That's what Dad said to me when I told him I was gay.

How can I not be what I am? Ignore the lean of my heart?
I've got over blaming you, Lord, for making me this way,
and begging you to make me someone else.
Now I'm struggling to accept the person I am.

It's a long and lonely project, to be honest.
I doubt I have your gift for celibacy, Lord.
I need more than verbal reassurances I am loved,
more than voices from on high, however mighty.

I need to be touched and held by someone I love.
I'm really afraid of ending up an old untouchable.
Is that the only future for me, Lord?

Lord, lover of life, giver of good things,

may your blessing be upon our food,
your grace be upon our family,
your kindness be upon our tongue.
May your peace, now and always,
find a home in our hearts.

And as we share our food,
may we share your love
not only among ourselves
but with all who hunger
for acceptance.

Amen.

BEFORE EATING TOGETHER

My beloved husband
calls me "the bag lady"

because I'm a shopaholic extraordinaire.
The other night he sat me down on the new leather sofa.
"Julia," he said, "can I share what I've been thinking?"
My heart sank at the prospect.

"Why do you envy what others have?" he asked.
"Why do you always have to go after bigger and better?
And when you get whatever it is – no matter what –
it never really satisfies that huge hunger of yours, love,
so you're off hunting for something else to want.

"Jealousy would be cheaper than envy, you know.
Why don't you get jealous of your sister Annie,
whom I adore, and demand that I give only you
exclusive total worship? At least
that wouldn't cost so much, my dear."

Of course, my dear hubby is right:
I don't do jealousy, but specialise in envy.
I'm sure our priest called envy a cardinal's sin,
so at least I'm in swanky company.

Why, oh why, Lord, am I always looking elsewhere,
ravenous to have what others do and I don't?
(I'm not really awfully religious, as you know,
and have missed Mass for the January sales.)
Can you help me see that what I have is more
than what I'll ever need and that what I want
will always be beyond me?

Help me to make my own the prayer of Saint Augustine:

"Late have I loved you,
O Beauty so ancient and so new,
late have I loved you!
You were within me, but I was outside,
and it was there that I searched for you.
I plunged into the lovely things which you created.
Created things kept me from you.

> *"You breathed your fragrance on me;*
> *I drew in breath and now I pant for you.*
> *I have tasted you, now I hunger and thirst for more.*
> *You touched me, and I burned for your peace."*

Are you, dear Lord of all creation,
the only one that can truly satisfy me?

Are parents really necessary, Lord?

I mean absolutely, without question?
Last night I heard Mum and Dad talking
in the kitchen about me and I got a real sense
they might be thinking of flogging me
to the highest bidder. Honest, no joke!

Everything I love, they seem to hate.
I love dinosaurs, playing in the dirt, fighting,
computer games, rock music, Manchester United.
They love cats, cleanliness, togetherness,
Scrabble, classical stuff, and cricket.
I mean this is serious! How can we carry on?

What's that big word I heard Dad use?
Oh yes, got it… Do you think we are compatible?
I mean can kids divorce their parents
because we've run out of being compatible?
It might have all started out okay, real fine and all,
but then things, you know, can get worse and worse.

I've talked to my guardian angel, but nothing back.
He's either on holiday or in hospital with broken wings,
worn ragged with all the stuff I tell him to take to you.
Which is why I'm going directly to the top with this one.

I know you must have enough on your plate at the moment,
but can you please sort us out, Lord? I mean if Mum and Dad
got to like computer games, I could have a go at Scrabble.
And if they could stand a bit of real rock
I might learn to hop to Mister Beethoven.

Can you get back to me, please, on this one, Lord?
Best regards to my vanished guardian angel, by the way.
Hope he got back okay. And I'd better say Amen.

HAVING TROUBLE AT HOME

Him (in the shed)

Dear God,
she keeps on at me, "Talk to me!"
and, as you know, I've never been fervent about words.
She wallpapers the house with language,
then wants to take the temperature of our relationship
every hour as if we're in intensive care.

"How do you think we're doing?"
Her question that haunts me round the house,
which is why I'm in the shed again, dear God.

I think we're doing fine, I tell her. I do, honestly.
She talks and I listen as attentively as I can;
she is the mouth and I am the ear;
she is word and I am receptive silence.
Isn't that a good relationship, Lord?
She must know I love her, surely,
and I never forget her birthday
or our wedding anniversary.

I love her to bits for who she is.
What more is there to say?

Her (in the bedroom)

We're at breaking point for sure, Lord,
and darling hubby doesn't seem to get it.
He is the dumbest man I know – literally.
Isn't he in love with eternal silence
and hopelessly suspicious of words?
Good job he's a plumber and not in the BBC.
I suspect he talks to his pipes and U-bends
more than to me. For a man who is a specialist
in unblocking drains, he is totally plugged himself.

> I can't bear it any more, Lord.
> I love him, of course, but living with him
> is like living in a Carthusian monastery
> where everyone has left except me.
> Doesn't he have my head dented?

Can't you do something? Quickly, please,
or all that stuff we promised "until death us do part"
will go straight down the drain.

DIFFERENCES IN MARRIED LIFE

I'm deeply happy,

Lord, to be who I am as a priest,
and grateful for the blessings it has brought me,
although, I must be honest, I feel ashamed of how
we have failed as a Church in the crisis of abuse.
On behalf of the Church I go down on my knees,
first to the people we have hurt and sorely damaged,
then to you, Lord, to acknowledge our sin,
our misuse of trust, and, yes, our violence.
Give us the grace to listen to our victims
as we are led to painful places we do not want to go to.
Let us listen, attentively, to their story of brokenness.

It might then seem too early to ask for mercy.

Mercy is not something any of us deserves;
it wouldn't be mercy if we deserved it.
Mercy is a gift from those who have been wronged,
not the right of those who have offended.
None of us has a right to walk away
after we have ruined someone's life.
We have to face honestly the consequences
of what we've done and the damage we've caused.
We have to pray and wait for long, for long,
for the gift of people's mercy.

As a priest I pray for a more humble Church, Lord,
that while we are justly proud of the faith we pass on,
we are self-reflective and honest about our own fragility.
What was it you said? "Among the pagans the rulers
lord it over them and make their authority felt.
This must not happen among you."

Help us never to lord it over others
but to be of real support to the people you send us.
I really love the Church I have served all my life,
which is why I pray that you might renew our confidence
in the liberating power of the Gospel
and deepen our joy in its service.

　FOR HUMILITY IN THE CHURCH

Most people think
I'm a thug

cos I wear a hoodie and have a Mohawk.
Uncle Chris is a Benedictine monk, and he looks
just like me with his black habit and hood,
but not as fit or as cool or anything!
As you must know, Lord –
you know everything, right? –
I'm the sweetest punk on the planet.

When I'm out in public, like the shopping centre,
I find it difficult to catch people's eye.
It's as if I'm going to head straight for them
and give them the Glasgow kiss, singing:

Love ain't like the movies
it blisters and bruises
and knocks you about with its fists.
It leaves you a wreckage
all postaged and packaged
and sealed with a Glasgow kiss.

I know the lyrics are not hymn number 345
but I love them and all, though they're not me.
I know I'm not an altar boy or anything,
but I just love this look – it's me, right?
Mum and Dad are fine about it, same with my girl,
although my sisters think I look a wreck.

You were trashed for your background,
your difference, the people you hung out with.
Did they ever gripe about your looks, Lord?

ON APPEARANCES

I was scared
about retirement,

Lord, the prospect of time seeming eternal,
and me, at home, an eternal fidget,
annoying the wife. Don't I hate golf?
Being in the building trade all my life,
I've worked outdoors and loved it,
the company of men and the good crack.

> With the daughter in the States
> and the son in Australia,
> we're very far from one another,
> and I miss them and the grandchildren.
> We follow them on that Facebook thing
> but it's never the same as a real hug, is it?
> It seems very lonely at times, dear Lord,
> just me, the wife, and the ocean.

Last week at Mass I smiled when I heard
the reader reciting the responsorial psalm,
something like: "Do not reject me
now that I am old and grey-headed.
I will take up the lyre and play until dawn."

> I won't be taking up guitar lessons
> and bore you with my singing, Lord.
> Haven't you enough to put up with already
> with our old parish choir, God love them!

Now, Lord, I have all the time in the world for you,
and I hope that you have some for me.
Keep me grateful for the wonderful life
and the family you have given to me.
Never take your loving hands away from them.

Sometimes, Lord, other people make a decision about you

over which you have no control,
and you are dumped with the consequences.
That happened to you, I know, in your passion
when you were abandoned, handed over, led away,
mocked, judged and finally condemned.
Nobody consulted you, did they?

> The Via Dolorosa has now come to my front door
> and I've been abandoned, mocked and condemned.
> My husband has decided to leave me
> for another woman – much younger, of course –
> and he can't contain his juvenile excitement
> as I can't contain my anger and frustration.

Before leaving me, he admitted, without a blush,
that he has had a string of affairs
throughout the thirty years of our marriage
because I was hopeless in the bed department.
This, I confess stupidly, was all news to me...

> New stuff, like this, can change the past – for ever.
> Now I realise that I got thirty years of my life wrong,
> thinking he had been faithful to me. How dumb!
> Thirty years is a long time to be wrong about
> what is under your own roof and in your own bed.
> In a stroke he has managed to disfigure
> every lovely memory I ever had of our married life.

Look at me now, Lord. What's to become of me?
Should I settle for the tomb, fix it up, make it snug
with a lick of paint here and there, discreet lighting,
perhaps new wallpaper? Help me, please, get out.

It's not often you see a sign on the door of a church,

warning people off. Oh dear Lord, this is my kind of parish church
that locks you out for the sake of your health!

These days at the doors of churches on a Sunday
you usually see an array of welcoming hostesses,
all smiles, pressing hymn books and improving leaflets
into your hand, ensuring that the church office has
your address, mobile number, e-mail and pyjama size.
I haven't darkened the door of a church
for about twenty years now. If I did go to church
I'd want to slink in, through a side door,
anonymously, as if I were a spy from out of town.

I still believe in you, Lord, as you know,
but I got exhausted with all the formality of church,
the awkward language, the antique feel of everything,
the endless droning, all that unheatable space,
to say nothing of the Neanderthal morality you hear.
Whole groups of people are banished to outer darkness
at the drop of a biretta. And we're never asked
what we think, expected only to nod and submit.

I think your agenda, Lord, has got lost along the way.

I don't criticise those who attend, but I don't buy
the trapped vision the Church preaches and teaches.
Honestly, I have a fierce admiration for how the churches
reach out to so many marginalised people
and I question what the banks and the corporations
and the clever professions do in the ghettos of the world.

I still feel more at home with a nun than a banker.

Your energy, Lord, was devoted to expressing
God's love for the world, preaching Good News,
helping orphans and widows, healing sick people,
and confronting religious pretence and legalism.

That agenda will never close down, will it?
There are so many, me included, still hungry
for what you hungered for, Lord. Keep us hungry
for your dream and never let us be parted from you.

Dear Lord, isn't she just the wee dote?

And I still have my earrings intact!

Being a grandmother is such a blessing,
since you don't have to do anything but be yourself.
The best time of my life is looking after Jackie,
and I can give her my undivided attention
and play daft games and sing silly songs –
and always offer a listening ear. Neither of us
is in a hurry, longing to be away somewhere else:
we don't have to squeeze each other into diaries.

As a Catholic granny I do have one wee worry –
the old biblical one: "What will this child turn out to be?"
Jackie's parents are "resting Catholics" –
having a bit of a break, they say, from organised religion.
They're wonderful people and loving parents,
and they did have Jackie baptised, though it stopped there.

I see grandmothers as the keepers of family history,
guiding lights to safe havens in these foggy times.
I've been teaching Jackie about you, Lord,
teaching her how to pray. Give her an attentive ear,
and let her know she is loved beyond the reaches
of our family, our history, this time, this world.

Let her know that she is not just our child but your child,
a child of God, dreamed from the foundation of the world.

I am a delicate soul, Lord, as you know,

and hate having my photograph taken,
so I've chosen this one of a beautiful ibex
I took on holiday. Hope you like it!

Haven't really got much to say, Lord –
have I ever? – just checking in with you,
hoping that you are bearing up today.
You know how I worry about you
with all that responsibility for the world
and everyone pestering you for something.
You must have a real imperial headache
most of eternity, Lord.

Hope, though, you don't still have a long rest
on our sabbath because that's when
we gather to honour you and hound you.
How are your Mondays?

Anyway, today is Valentine's Day, Lord,
and I just thought I'd send a loving thought.
I know you get a bad press in many places
and blamed for everything that goes wrong,
from a case of hiccups to a tsunami.

This is just to say I love you.
Thank you, Lord, for loving me first,
for giving me such weird and wonderful friends,
and for blessing me with such a bizarre family.
Can I pray for those who are lonely and unloved
that you might send them a wicked surprise
this Valentine's Day? Go on, you can do it!

ON VALENTINE'S DAY

This is my favourite wedding photograph

among the hundreds that were taken that day
back in Clydebank on the thirteenth of April 1971.
A friend took it to remind me for ever
of my last moment of freedom
before Danny slipped on the wedding ring!

That was thirty-eight years ago today,
and our fingers are now a bit crooked, Lord.
I love this photograph because it marks
the real beginning of my story and Danny's;
it celebrates the start of our journey together
and the people the two of us have become,
both still holding on to each other tightly.

Thank you, Lord, for the gift of this quiet man,
who has stuck by me through thick and thin
with a tenderness that must be borrowed from you.
Thank you for our three grown-up children –
Daniel, Denis, and Susan – who are a delight;
for Antoinette and Annette and our grandchildren,
Daniel, Molly, and the newly arrived Matthew.
They are all within shouting distance of home,
and, Lord God, do they shout. Haven't they
got my poor head wrecked at times!

My gratitude is not for things but for people,
and I could add to the litany for ever and a day.

My prayer is one you have heard before, Lord:
"Stay with us; it is nearly evening
and the day is almost over."

ON A WEDDING ANNIVERSARY

Hi dear Lord,
it's me again,

as if you don't recognise my shape, my voice,
my accent, my cautious whispers.

> You know that confessing to you alone is not fashionable;
> should really do it now on reality TV or on some talk show.
> True confessions need a live audience, loud lusty reactions
> between thrill and outrage. Usually applause follows rather
> than a muttered penance, in the box, of three Hail Marys.

I guess the promotional value of exposing your sins in public
outweighs the shame of having them revealed by others.
Even a miniature celebrity can get famous for interesting sins.
Confession really pays: papers sell; magazines shout.

> Sorry, I divert as usual – my hopeless old habit –
> anything but confronting my own personal weakness.

Yet again I ask you, Lord, to forgive my narcissism,
my everlasting obsession with myself and my tiny world,
my pride, my reluctance to face up to my own faults
while being ever alert to others' shortcomings.
Why are my eyes and ears primed for others' mistakes?

> Forgive my oft-declared interest in other people,
> my pronounced enthusiasm for the details of their life,
> while knowing most of them don't really matter a hoot.
> Forgive my inability to notice what is happening
> beyond the range of my bathroom mirror.

Take away my self-adhesiveness, Lord.
Replace my self-conceit with some real passion.
Please give me part of your sacred heart for others,
a special tenderness even for one human being.
Let someone's love redeem me, please,
from stubborn satisfaction with myself.

She smiles all the time, Mum does,

waves and says hello to everyone she meets,
indiscriminate in her devotion to the human race.
Of course the poor soul has no idea who anyone is,
including me, her only daughter.
I've put piles of photos by her bedside in the home,
to fight forgetfulness, but every time I come to visit,
the adventure begins again.

God, we do this dreary walk every week –
down to the town for coffee and back again –
but for Mum the landscape is full of wonder
and everything is startlingly new.
She never looks me in the eyes,
as if aware nothing will register there,
so her eyes are always roaming around
absorbing what appears forever fresh.

The pain is mine, of course, not hers:
to love without recognition;
to be faithful without return;
to persevere in times of trial.

Sometimes I wonder, Lord,
if this is the story of your life with us.
As your love accepts us unconditionally,
help me to appreciate Mum as she is now.

Let me love her in her fragility, accept
the joy she brings to everyone she meets.
Let me stay by her faithfully until
the day she sees you, face to face,
in final joyful recognition.

FOR AN ELDERLY PARENT

You become a sharp observer of people, Lord,

sitting on the street all day long – what else to do?
My talent is to make most people uncomfortable
as if I'm proof positive you can screw up your life
and end up in the gutter, alone. Some prophet, I am!
I know I should get a dog to attract more sympathy,
but I can hardly feed myself as it is.

Were there any dogs at the crucifixion?

Most passers-by avoid eye contact and quicken pace
like they've just remembered where to go.
Others glance down, see only a bottle of water,
and think about working up a smile when
it's already too late. A few growl advice
like they're certified psychiatrists on the run.
Fewer pay any attention at all.
Not that I bother, because, to be honest, Lord,
I'd probably pass by me as well.

I do a lot of praying, as you know –
half the time I don't know if I'm talking to you
or wittering away to myself. Does it matter?

I do believe, in my bones, that one day
you will pass this way but not pass me by.
I'm content to wait for that day – I mean
it's not like I've anywhere to go or anything.
Like you, I have all the time in the world.

I've spent all my life
on the missions –

in Kenya, in Zimbabwe, in Borneo –
and now I've come reluctantly home, to die.
How I have treasured my life wherever
I've been sent, especially the poor people
I was privileged to nurse along the way.

> Dear Master, I know why you love the poor
> and the sinners – aren't they altogether
> much nicer to be around all day?
> I've never had to struggle for their acceptance,
> nor they for mine: weren't we made for each other?
> For sure it was tough and raw at times –
> sometimes, it has to be said, even dangerous –
> but didn't we have the time of our lives?

I wouldn't change those times for anything.
Nowadays I try to hand over to our young sisters
what I myself received, in the hope that they
will learn to reverence and serve
the kind of people you especially love.

> Now the time has come for me to be nursed
> and I've promised not to give any grief.
> Keep me from being cranky or pernickety,
> and never let me lose my sense of humour.
> As you called me in life, Lord, welcome me
> into your loving arms when you call me at last.

I know my smile is too energetic for some, my laugh too loud,

my face too round, my speech too slow, my eyes too slanted,
my heart too weak. And, apparently, I'm too affectionate…
Dear God, apart from all that, I'm really fine! By now I know
I'm different from most people, but I'm just normal to my family,
although sometimes at school I get called "stupid mongo" and stuff.

I asked Mum about the word mongo,
and she said that people like me
used to be known as Mongoloids.
She smiled and then continued dusting.
That was it. No further explanation.
(Mum's not given to wasting words.)

So I dashed upstairs and Googled "mongoloid" –
to discover that "the World Health Organization
officially dropped references to mongolism in 1965
after a request by the Mongolian delegate".
The poor guy was upset having all us unwanted citizens,
without proper passports, craving access to Mongolia!

I know I frighten some people because
they don't know what to say to me or how to respond.
When I go to Mass with Mum or to the supermarket,
it's often a case of: "Does he take sugar?"
Some people just bypass me, presuming I'm a dummy,
without feeling or intelligence or preferences or prejudices.

Dearest Lord, give me patience with "normal" people:
help me to understand their slowness, their coolness,
their nervousness and their really dismal manners.
Except Mum and Dad and Auntie Ellen, of course!

ON HAVING DOWN'S SYNDROME

"Out of his infinite glory,

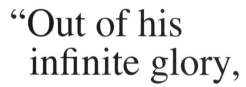

may God give you the power through his Spirit
for your hidden self to grow strong."

This is my favourite prayer – for my hidden self.
I guess, Lord, you don't hear too many prayers
from the likes of me. No one knows who
I really am except my controller and you –
not my wife, my kids, my parents. Nobody.

As an intelligence officer (some say spy)
I'm trained as an excellent conversationalist
in five languages, to gather information.
I watch; I wait; I listen; I leave; I report.
No information is considered irrelevant.
I never draw attention to myself, making
the background my natural habitat.
Nobody would notice me even on an empty beach.

There are times, Lord, when I get tired
of being my cover, forever hiding who I am
and what I do, exhausted with the tension
generated by prolonged deception.
Sometimes I wonder if I know who I really am.

I know I shouldn't be talking even to you, but,
so far, there's no device for tapping silent prayer.
Keep me, Lord, in conversation with you;
otherwise I might lose the little of me that is left.

FOR MY HIDDEN SELF

Teach us,

Lord, not only how to pray
but how to play. Many of us have forgotten;
too many of us, sadly, have never learned.
If no one ever died whispering a last regret
that they didn't spent more time in the office,
or on the shop floor, or wherever they worked,
how come we are so slow to understand?

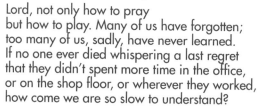

Help us to learn from horses and dolphins,
from solemn giraffes and silly puppy dogs –
to lavish time, uselessly, foolishly,
in each other's company. Who knows?
If we did that, we might even learn
to squander time with you, Lord.

We hallow your name, dear Father,

and the names of all who have gone
before us in this life.
Give rest and peace to your servants.
Grant sanctuary to our fathers and mothers,
to all our kinsfolk and friends,
and to all peoples who have lived by faith
and passed by a thousand ways
on their road to your eternal presence.

Eternal rest grant unto them, O Lord,
and let perpetual light shine upon them.
May they rest in peace.

Amen.

FOR THE DEAD

We're having our
first holiday in years

to celebrate our new liberation
with our youngest leaving home.
God, did he take his time!
"Sean," we said, "you're twenty-eight
and need to get going with your own life.
We're not tossing you out – we love you –
just encouraging you, son, to make a start."

"Oh," he said, "you'll really miss me
when I'm gone, leaving you two pottering around
in the empty nest. Are you really sure about this?
I mean – really?" We laughed and assured him.
He's got his own place now, thank God.

For a break, I thought the Yorkshire Dales,
but Sue said we need to be more adventurous.
So here we are, on a snowy runway in Finland,
the best bargain she could find among
the "Quick Getaways" in the travel agent's.

In a way it doesn't matter where we are,
even in an empty nest, as long as we're together.
Keep us close together, Lord, and strong;
let us never turn away from each other, ever.
Help our love to deepen, our kindness increase;
and please, please ensure Sean can pay his rent.

WHEN THE NEST IS EMPTY

This is the job he
hates most as a soldier –

being "tourist fodder" he calls it – on duty at Horse Guards,
all decked up and nowhere to go. Wish he was there now,
instead of being on tour so far away, on the dark side,
in southern Helmand Province, Afghanistan.

> Stephen has wanted to be only one thing, a soldier,
> serving Queen and country, and he takes great pride
> in who he is, in his own comrades, and what they do.
> It has, I admit, been the making of him,
> although I now spend my life worrying about him.

No mother wants to see her son go into harm's way,
however grand the cause might be. Above all,
we want security and safety for our children,
and we pray, whatever they might become,
that they will grow up far from danger.
We really respect Stephen's choice and life,
but not an hour of any day or night goes by
that I don't imagine the worst. Stephen jokes with me:
"Oh Mum, you have a thing for catastrophic thinking!"

> To say as he leaves, "Look after yourself, son," sounds
> so feeble as you're left with the echo of your own voice.
> Will you please look after him for me, Lord?
> Will his love and goodness be a shield against bullets
> and roadside bombs when he's out on foot patrol?
> He keeps saying to me, as if it's his mantra:
> "Oh Mum, it's not about how good you are but how lucky."

Preserve him, Lord, in your safekeeping. Bring him home.
Let's all see him again, trying his best not to smile or to wink,
when we visit him on duty at Horse Guards.

FOR MY SOLDIER SON

Richard and I recently moved in here, number 59,

our first house, more than we could really afford.
When we first went to see it, we knew it had been empty
for yonks, but we never expected such total dereliction.

> The estate agents, skilled in dazzling description,
> had advertised it as "a spacious residential space
> that might, in time, require some sensitive restoration.
> The many original features throughout the house
> are bound to delight the discerning buyer. Must see."

We were truly appalled at the wreck of what we saw,
baffled at what the original features were throughout;
but Rich reckoned, given our tight budget,
it was all we could afford and that, as a builder,
he could make it all good, as hinted, in time.

> He's done fantastic work! But the real plus here
> are the neighbours – none, thank God, from hell –
> who've welcomed us with open arms and teacakes.

I can't tell you, Lord, after life in the big city,
what it means to have real neighbours
who don't have your e-mail but know your name,
who're not on Twitter but actually talk to you.
It's so glorious after the anonymity of where we were.

> Thanks, Lord, for all the unexpected kindnesses,
> for old-fashioned civility and for chatting over the hedge.
> May we both be happy where we've landed now,
> and have a sense of belonging somewhere at last.

I don't talk to
you, Lord,
as often as I used to

because I doubt you're really in charge of anything.
So what's the point of praying to you?
I used to think that what happened in the world
happened because of your attention and kindness –
providence was the big word we learned in school –
but I don't believe that stuff any more.

> I think you're as feeble as I am,
> powerless to change anything.

I've run out of tears for those I have lost –
Mum and Dad, my two brothers and three sisters.
I was late coming home from school that day,
arrived after what happened, to see my family
spread around our house, macheted into pieces.
That day we belonged to the wrong tribe.
That day you were nowhere around.

I ran away and have been running ever since.
I don't tell anyone who I am or where I'm from –
I act dumb all the time because I trust no one.
Never will. Not even you. I want to survive.

I'd pray for help, Lord, if I thought it would
make any difference. I'm just keeping you up
with where I am. I'm in my third refugee camp.
I wash the soldiers' uniforms and get food for sex.
I'm managing. I'm surviving. I'm still here.

Where are you?

She really brightens up this hospital –

Dr Sarah Hutchinson, everyone's favourite.
When she smiles, your pain diminishes;
when she talks to you, it's like being addressed,
at last, by your unforthcoming guardian angel.
I've never been in the company of anyone
whose presence is so attentive and healing.
You could learn from her, Lord, honestly.

That said, this place reminds me of school,
with the long corridors, the high windows,
the uniforms, the crêpe soles, the strong smell
of disinfectant, and the fear you'll never get out alive.

I must say the doctors and nurses
are unwearied in their care. The only thing
I hate is when the consultant comes around,
followed by a flock of fretting students,
and has a seminar at the bottom of your bed
as if you're an entry in a medical dictionary.
Wish they'd say something – even just wave.

Anyway, Lord, I'm really lucky to be here.
I'd like to pray for all doctors and nurses,
even for medical students, that you might
grant them skill and devotion in their work,
gentleness and patience with all of us.
Guide their minds, their hearts and their hands
in the heroic work they do for our salvation.

Amen.

Hi, God,
meet my best friend

with the droopy ears and eyes.
His name is Hulk cos he's huge.
He really looks after me,
even when I'm in a bad mood,
and stays with me wherever I go.

If you're as nice, then I'm okay.

Will you please look after him
and stop him from getting old?
Thanks. Got to get back for tea
or Mum will really kill us.

FOR MY DOG

Am in the wilds of Donegal,

on the west coast of Ireland,
uncovering my roots, trying to access the family tree
which goes way down deep. Coming from Los Angeles,
I never realised, until now, that my origins were fastened
to such raw beauty of mountain and rock and loch and sea.
For sure, Lord, you took your time crafting this place.

Thanks, Lord, for giving me a sense of belonging
not only to a gentle people but to a wild landscape,
a mysterious combination I've come to love:
may I find that exotic mix in my own soul.
As the last in our long line, let me pass on this gift
so that our ancient family tree might bloom again.

AT THE END OF THE LINE

"Through him all things came to be.

Not one thing had its being but through him."

Just to say, Lord of all life and light,
a small thank you for the unfolding beauty of life
and for all we take for granted every day.
If none of us managed ourselves into existence,
our whole life is total gift, isn't it?
Who we are is what we owe to others.

With full heart I would like to express thanks
for all you have bequeathed us in life,
for the stunning inheritance we have received.
For the breath we take, for the light of our eyes,
for the gift of speech, for the ability to move,
for the talent to think, to imagine, to dream,
and above all for the capacity to love others
and get lucky when we're loved in return.

For the total diversity of your creation:
for different lands and oceans and skies;
for countless races and colours and tongues;
for all religions who strive to revere you
and for all people who cannot manage belief.

For the multitude of various animals
that share our world on land and in sea;
for trees and plants and flowers –
especially, for me, the Japanese maple!

For all this, and so much more,
a thousand thanks, dear Lord.

FOR THE GIFT OF LIFE

Whoever told me time would heal was lying;

whoever said I'd surely overcome the loss
was hopelessly off-key. When Mark was around
I could forget him, casually, for a while;
now he's gone, he's everywhere I go.

> I've tried going only to places
> we haven't been together, but his absence
> dominates the restaurant, the gallery,
> the cathedral, the city, even the country.
> Wherever I go, his absence is more real,
> much larger, somehow, than everyone there.

It's been three years now – Mum and Dad
tell me I'm into overtime, and soon I'll be free.
I'm not sure I want to be free. For what?
I miss him, I love him, I yearn for him.
My whole body and spirit cleaves to him.
The vow we made – "Till death us do part" –
hasn't worked in our case, has it?

> I don't ask, dear Lord, that you release me
> and let me love again. I don't know, in truth,
> what to pray for any more. Except to thank you
> for the love you sent me; for letting me
> taste the world, for so short a while, with him.

IN LOVING MEMORY

We gather at this sacred time –

the eleventh hour of the eleventh day
of the eleventh month –
on the anniversary of Armistice Day, 1918,
the day so many hungered to believe
that this was "the war to end all wars".

> We who gather share their hunger
> but not, sadly, their belief:
> that war has yet to be fought.

We remember all those who have died
for freedom and justice in the field of conflict.
We hold their names holy before the Lord.

> We call to mind the love and generosity
> that led them to give their life, their all,
> so that others might live in safety and peace.
> May their dying not be in vain.

Help us, Lord, to honour their sacrifice:
to love stubbornly and for long,
that there might indeed be an end to war.
Let our love be the best homage we give
to all who sacrificed their lives for us.

> May they rest in peace.

> Amen.

ON REMEMBRANCE DAY

Also published by Redemptorist Publications

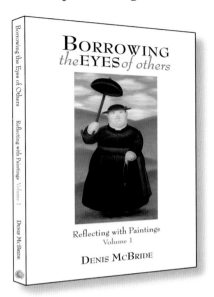

Borrowing the Eyes of Others
Reflecting with Paintings 1

Using works by artists as varied as Giorgione, Magritte, Cézanne, Van Gogh, and others, as well as some who are less well known, Denis McBride brings the depicted characters and scenes dramatically to life, and speaks through them to us – the onlookers, the casual observers, the passers-by. During these often-strange encounters we are invited to pause and listen to what they each have to say. In doing this, the author hopes we will relate the voices we hear to the way we understand and live our life.

Finest characters you will meet
As a psychiatrist, you don't expect your patients to bring you reading to improve your sympathy and understanding. I was given this book written by a priest – I don't read priests – and got caught up in the life of these wonderful weird characters.

Whoever the author is he is much more than a priest, unusually sharp about personality insight and contradiction, not only between characters but within characters. Not only does he write beautifully, but sees people with reverence, however imperfect and flawed. In this he is my teacher.

Yes, I have learned from this book and am learning to love it, but it does make my usual clients rather dull.

Dr M. Lincoln

ISBN 978-0-85231-351-0

For pricing information or to order:

PHONE: 01420 88222 | EMAIL: sales@rpbooks.co.uk | ONLINE: www.rpbooks.co.uk

Awakening to Yourself
Reflecting with Paintings 2

A second volume of Denis McBride's thought-provoking reflections on paintings. Each painting and narrative provides an opportunity to encounter God, ourselves and others more deeply. Readers will be surprised at how the stories touch them and how they highlight some of today's moral, ethical and religious issues.

Brilliant imagination!
What a brilliant imagination! I wish I could dream and see like this! Really looked forward to this book after the first volume, and it did not disappoint. My favourite was Saint Joseph sharing his story, seeing how he handled all the interruptions in his life. I loved the insight that developed with this human story, and it really made me reflect on the importance of the interruptions in my own life.

Fr McBride has a clever way of getting you to look at someone else, reflect on their story, and suddenly you realise you are thrown back on your own. How gentle and discreet is that?

Neil MacDonald

ISBN 978-0-85231-361-9

For pricing information or to order:

PHONE: 01420 88222 | EMAIL: sales@rpbooks.co.uk | ONLINE: www.rpbooks.co.uk

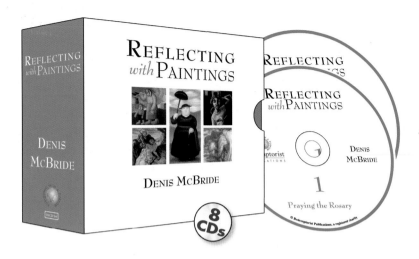

Reflecting with Paintings – 15 voices from both volumes

In his series *Reflecting with Paintings* Fr Denis McBride takes us on a fascinating and challenging journey of imagination. The various works of art featured are used to open up a conversation between the human story and that of Christ. Anyone who has heard Fr McBride speak will be delighted to hear that the narratives are now available on CD. (Copies of the paintings are included.)

How to listen to stories

I received these CDs from a colleague in London: wah-wah, what a gift I have gotten! Voices communicate so much more than the written word. These CDs are a breathtaking assortment of voices, eager to share their story. Of course there is only one voice – that of Fr Denis McBride – but his ability to overhear the stories of others, catch the colour of people's pain and their joy, and then communicate that with passion is such a rare gift. I have heard my own restless voice speaking from this assembly, which sometimes frightened me but more often delighted with its understated British humour.

Before people speak, they should listen – I mean really listen to other people rather than just react to what they think they hear. As a counsellor I know that listening to people is exhausting – and rewarding. Fr Denis must be one of the best listeners in the world and one of the sharpest observers of human behaviour. Before his voice speaks, everything is first in his attentive eye and ear, in the observed detail. I need to get him out here to teach class!

No one is beyond the reach of his understanding, no matter how odd they are or how screwball. Every voice gets a sympathetic hearing, which is the nearest I have come to recognising the Gospel of our Lord Jesus Christ. I'm going to use these tapes for my college students, to help them pay attention to different stories and hear and hear again the lone voice that pleads for understanding. And then listen again. And then some.

Dr Craig McKenzie (California)

For pricing information or to order:

PHONE: 01420 88222 | EMAIL: sales@rpbooks.co.uk | ONLINE: www.rpbooks.co.uk